I0814865

Sports Strategies

AUTO RACING STRATEGIES

BY ANTHONY K. HEWSON

An Imprint of Abdo Publishing
abdobooks.com

abdobooks.com

Published by Abdo Publishing, a division of ABDO, PO Box 398166, Minneapolis, Minnesota 55439.

Printed in the United States of America, North Mankato, Minnesota.
102023
012024

Cover Photos: Rudy Carezzevoli/Getty Images Sport/Getty Images (left); Angela Weiss/AFP/Getty Images (right)
Interior Photos: Josep Lago/AFP/Getty Images, 5; Robert Laberge/Getty Images Sport/Getty Images, 6–7, 23; RacingOne/ISC Archives/Getty Images, 9, 38–39; Brian Lawdermilk/Getty Images Sport/Getty Images, 10; Jared C. Tilton/Getty Images Sport/Getty Images, 12–13; Jeffrey Vest/Icon Sportswire/Getty Images, 14–15; Stacy Revere/Getty Images Sport/Getty Images, 16–17; Michael Allio/Icon Sportswire/Getty Images, 19, 24–25; Adam Lacy/Icon Sportswire/Getty Images, 20; Matthew Pearce/Icon Sportswire/Getty Images, 21; Paul-Henri Cahier/Hulton Archive/Getty Images, 26–27; Dan Istitene/Formula 1/Getty Images, 29; Eric Gaillard/Pool/AFP/Getty Images, 30–31; Shutterstock Images, 32; Qian Jun/MB Media/Getty Images Sport/Getty Images, 34–35; Joe Portlock/Formula 1/Getty Images, 36; OFF/AFP/Getty Images, 41; Steven Markham/Icon Sportswire/Getty Images, 43; James Gilbert/Getty Images Sport/Getty Images, 45

Editors: Charlie Beattie and Patrick Donnelly
Series Designer: Joshua Olson

Library of Congress Control Number: 2023939423

Publisher's Cataloging-in-Publication Data

Names: Hewson, Anthony K., author.
Title: Auto racing strategies / by Anthony K. Hewson
Description: Minneapolis, Minnesota: Abdo Publishing, 2024 | Series: Sports strategies | Includes online resources and index.
Identifiers: ISBN 9781098292416 (lib. bdg.) | ISBN 9798384910350 (ebook)
Subjects: LCSH: Sports teams--Juvenile literature. | Teamwork (Sports)--Juvenile literature. | Athletes--Training of--Juvenile literature. | Automobiles, Racing--Juvenile literature.
Classification: DDC 796.01--dc23

TABLE OF CONTENTS

INTRODUCTION

The goal of every auto race is the same—be the fastest and finish first. But being the fastest is about more than just putting the pedal to the floor. Strategy is what makes auto racing so exciting. The right decision at the right time can mean the difference between winning and losing.

Not all racing series are created equal, even if they might look like it. IndyCar and Formula One both feature open-wheel cars with a driver's compartment open to the air. But while IndyCars are all built using the same basic components, each Formula One team manufactures its car from scratch.

The stock cars used in NASCAR races may look like road cars. But they are instead purpose-built race cars that come with their own unique challenges. They go through tires quickly. And they run on high-speed, oval-shaped tracks where aerodynamics is everything.

One form of motorsports where speed isn't everything is endurance racing. The fastest car wins, but only the cars that can survive races that can take up to an entire day will even have a chance. Here, speed takes a back seat to strategy as the race progresses.

It takes more than just a fast car to win a race. Drivers are constantly making decisions throughout a race to try to gain an edge.

PIRELLI
PIRELLI
PIRELLI
PIRELLI
PETRONAS
cognizant
PETRONAS

Chapter 1

NASCAR

Either Chase Elliott or Martin Truex Jr. was going to win the 2018 NASCAR Cup Series race in Watkins Glen, New York. The drivers were battling back and forth for the lead as the race neared its completion. And each was hoping he would have enough fuel to finish.

Truex's team was one of the best at managing fuel mileage. Over long races, refueling stops are necessary. However, each stop wastes valuable time that could be spent on the track. Teams that can stop

Chase Elliott (9) keeps ahead of Martin Truex Jr. at the 2018 NASCAR Cup Series race in Watkins Glen, New York.

78
CAMRY
MONSTER
9

as few times as possible put themselves in the best position to win a race.

Both Truex and Elliott believed they had just enough fuel to finish the race. At the start of the final lap, Truex tried to pass Elliott. But soon Truex's engine started to sputter. He was out of fuel. Elliott raced away to his first Cup Series victory. Soon after crossing the finish line, he ran out of gas himself. He needed to be pushed into Victory Lane. But all that mattered was that he had crossed the finish line. Pit stop strategy makes for a fine line between winning and losing.

TIME OFF TRACK

Stops for repairs have been a part of racing from the very beginning. But those early stops took ages compared with the coordinated, efficient pit stops of today. In the 1960s, the Wood Brothers NASCAR team came up with a way to speed things up.

The Wood Brothers gave each crew member a specific role. Then they practiced their stops to remove any wasted time. They also built their own lightweight equipment so they could move quickly around the car. The modern pit stop evolved from those changes. NASCAR stops that used to take more than a minute now can take less than 10 seconds.

Ten seconds might not sound like a long time, but NASCAR teams stop several times per race. Being even a second slow

Driver Cale Yarborough, *center*, poses with the Wood brothers, *from left*, Clay, Glen, Leonard, and Delano, before a NASCAR race in 1967.

each time can add up. Those extra seconds can ruin a team's chances at winning.

Fuel is one of the factors teams must consider during stops. But like any race car, stock cars rely on good grip of the track to go as fast as possible. As a race goes on, the car's tires wear out. Teams that pit more often can keep fresh tires. Teams that pit less often might risk slowing the car down on worn tires.

One compromise teams sometimes make is choosing to change two tires instead of all four. This gives the car a

A crew member makes a wedge adjustment on Carl Edwards's car during a race in 2015.

bit more grip while cutting the time on pit road roughly in half. However, if one team changes two tires and its closest competitor changes four, the other car will travel faster. That could help them make up for any lost time on pit road. Because of this, a key part of a team's decision-making is guessing what its opponents will do.

While teams are changing tires, they are usually also adding fuel. The more fuel a team adds to the car, the longer the pit stop takes. But that's just one consideration teams must make. Too much fuel can make a car heavy and slow. Teams want to add just enough to maintain speed without running out of fuel too soon.

Tire grip and fuel weight are a couple of the ways a car changes throughout a race. These changes might affect the way a car handles. Teams have one major adjustment they can make during a pit stop, called a wedge adjustment.

A wedge adjustment turns a screw that compresses or loosens the spring on a stock car's rear suspension. Compressing the spring means the car will bounce less and stay tighter to the track. A looser suspension means the car can absorb bumps better on rougher surfaces. The particular conditions of a race and track determine what kind of adjustment a driver calls for.

In 2022 Kyle Busch's Joe Gibbs Racing team set an all-time pit stop record of 8.96 seconds. His crew had long been known as one of the best in NASCAR. Their skills and efficiency helped Busch take home NASCAR Cup championships in both 2015 and 2019.

Pit Road Athletes

Changing tires and filling fuel are not specialized jobs, so NASCAR teams don't need trained mechanics for pit stops. Instead, they often hire former athletes from other sports who can do the work quickly. Football players, soccer players, track-and-field competitors, and more have made second careers helping shave time off NASCAR pit stops.

BACK ON TRACK

A lot of strategy is rolled into pit stops, when cars are taking a break from the race. But plenty of strategy goes into on-track performance as well. NASCAR drivers compete against one another to win, but they also belong to teams consisting of several cars. Working together with teammates can help all drivers from that team get to the front of the pack.

Stock cars are heavily influenced by aerodynamics acting on the car. The cars run at high speeds, usually on oval-shaped tracks, with cars bunched together in packs. A line of cars moves as one unit, with the lead car punching a hole in the air and the other cars following behind. But one car out on its own has to move that air by itself with nobody "pushing" from behind. Racing directly in front of, or behind, a teammate can help both cars manage that resistance.

Racing directly behind another car, or "drafting," can help a driver stay fast while saving fuel.

McDonald's
23
MENARDS
12
18

Hendrick cars.com
NASCAR
SIEMENS
Hendrick
cars.com

Drivers find their teammates on the track with the help of a spotter or the team's crew chief. The spotter stands high above the track and lets a driver know which cars are in their area and any danger to look out for. If a driver knows a teammate's car is nearby, that helps them know where to make a move.

Teams also have one eye on the season standings whenever they make an in-race strategic decision. In addition to receiving points based on where they finish, teams can also earn points at the conclusion of each stage of a race. NASCAR introduced stages in 2017, and that introduced a new element of strategy. The stages break each race up into three or four smaller pieces. Drivers who win one of those pieces earn points toward their season totals. Teams have to decide whether they want to go for an overall win or a top finish in a stage. That decision can potentially change their pitting strategy for the rest of the race.

A crew chief watches over a team and relays instructions to the driver on the track.

Chapter 2

IndyCar

Romain Grosjean found himself well behind the leaders early in the 2021 Grand Prix of Indianapolis. But like all IndyCar drivers, Grosjean had a weapon to help him battle his way toward the front. All IndyCars are equipped with a system called "push to pass." It's triggered by a button on the car's steering wheel that gives a racer a temporary boost of horsepower.

The system isn't always available. Racers are limited to 200 seconds of boost per race. At Indianapolis, Grosjean needed all his passes just to overtake Colton Herta and

Romain Grosjean rounds a corner at the 2021 Grand Prix of Indianapolis.

valpak
#Nurtec ODT
#Nurtec ODT
ENEOS MOTOR OIL
valpak

get back to the second position. But having run out of push-to-pass options by then, Grosjean couldn't overtake leader Will Power. Grosjean had to settle for second place.

Still, Grosjean's choice to use up his passes early proved to be a wise strategic choice. Without doing so, he might never have had the chance to get back among the leaders. Those are the types of decisions IndyCar drivers face on each exciting weekend.

Strategy is especially important in a series such as IndyCar. More than in most racing series, the entries in an IndyCar race share a lot of similarities. Teams all must use the same chassis. And they have the choice of just two engine manufacturers. This leads to close, competitive racing where every decision counts.

IN-RACE CALLS

The basic setup of an IndyCar is determined by the type of track. There is one setup for oval tracks and one setup for road courses. The series even has a special set of tires used only on oval tracks.

Road courses offer more tire options. Teams must decide between softer tires that have more grip but wear out quickly, or harder tires that last longer but are not as fast. They also have rain tires for wet conditions on road courses. Rain tires

Red-striped tires, known as "Alternate Red," are made of a softer compound that allows for faster cornering in IndyCar.

wear out fast on a dry track, so teams have to be careful to fit them only if the race will be run in wet conditions.

Whichever tires are used, another important decision in each race is when to change them. The factors teams look at include how long the race is, how quickly they expect tires to wear out, what kind of fuel mileage they expect, and more. A team might develop a strategy thinking they can complete a race using only a certain number of pit stops. But things can change quickly in a race. A team must be ready to shift to a different plan if it has to make an unexpected stop.

The marshal waves a yellow caution flag at the 2018 Indianapolis 500.

In racing, a yellow caution flag comes out to signal a collision or hazardous conditions on the track. In comparison with NASCAR, IndyCar races have fewer caution flags. That can make things tricky. Pitting under a caution flag allows a car to stay on the lead lap. But teams that pit while the race is in full swing risk falling behind.

Sometimes tires perform differently than expected. If they wear out more quickly, teams might decide it is worth it to make an extra stop to change a bad tire. Or if a set of tires gets better performance than expected, that could reduce the need for stops.

Opponents' strategies can be influential too. Drivers do not want to pit on their own. Race cars run faster when in groups of two or more, so ideally a driver would stop with other cars. A team may choose to pit earlier than planned if it sees that other cars are stopping.

Unlike most other open-wheel series, IndyCar competes on oval tracks and road courses. The pit stop strategy for both

Romain Grosjean's crew executes a pit stop at the Texas Motor Speedway during a 2023 race.

kinds of tracks is different. Oval tracks are much shorter, so cars sitting on pit road will lose more time than they would on a road course. This makes it even more important to pit with other cars and to take advantage of caution periods.

IN THE DRIVER'S HANDS

In most cars, a steering wheel is a pretty simple device. But in IndyCar, the driver's wheel is covered by an array of buttons, knobs, and screens. They give IndyCar drivers several strategic options right at their fingertips.

There are a few adjustments a driver can make to improve the handling of the car. They can change the weight distribution to help the car handle better when turning. Another option can either loosen or tighten the car's suspension. Both adjustments are important, as the car's handling changes due to tire wear and fuel loss. Drivers can also change the flow of fuel, depending on whether they want maximum power or need to save gas.

Perhaps the most unique strategy available to IndyCar drivers involves the push-to-pass system. It makes an extra 60 horsepower available at the push of a button. As a typical IndyCar engine generates 550 to 700 horsepower, this is a boost of about 10 percent. Though "pass" is in the name, drivers don't have to use it only for passing.

IndyCar drivers can control many aspects of their cars from their steering wheels.

This boost comes with limits. Drivers may use it only after two green flag laps. And they can use it for a total of only 200 seconds in an entire race. Like Grosjean in 2021, drivers must decide when they need it the most.

The IndyCar schedule presents interesting strategic choices. While many of the series' stars run all the races, some teams opt to have drivers who specialize in either ovals or road courses. Drivers such as Grosjean who got their start in Formula One are typically more used to road courses. But drivers such as Jimmie Johnson who come from stock cars have more experience with ovals.

Carb Day

Strategy in IndyCar used to be a bit more complicated. The final practice session before the Indianapolis 500 is known as "Carburetion Day" or "Carb Day." A carburetor is a device that mixes fuel and air before it is burned in an engine. Getting this mix just right was difficult but crucial for making an engine run correctly. Though IndyCars haven't used carburetors since the 1960s, the name continues as a nod to the past.

Teams also have multiple cars. Sometimes they can try different strategies during the same race. At the 2019 Honda Indy 200, Arrows teammates Marcus Ericsson and James Hinchcliffe qualified in spots that started side by side on the grid. The team then decided to run each car with different tire compounds to see which worked better. Neither driver ultimately did well in the race, but those are the kinds of decisions that can decide an IndyCar race.

Having multiple cars in a race gives a team a chance to try out different race strategies.

mission
VELO
LUCAS OIL
ARROW
mission
ARROW
ARROW

Chapter 3

Formula One

Everything was going great for Rubens Barrichello at the 2001 Malaysian Grand Prix. He was running third, and his Ferrari teammate, Michael Schumacher, was right there with him. Both drivers had a chance to finish on the podium.

Suddenly, rain started to fall. Ferrari called both drivers into the pits to change tires, one after the other. But Barrichello's tires weren't ready. He had to wait in his car while his tires were found and fitted. During the delay, Barrichello dropped to 11th place.

Rubens Barrichello, *left*, and Michael Schumacher, *right*, fly down a straight during the rainy 2001 Malaysian Grand Prix.

Barrichello recovered to finish second, but he certainly could've won if not for the mistake. Sometimes even the best race plan is ruined by an unexpected problem.

Formula One is considered the most technologically advanced racing series in the world. Teams spend hundreds of millions of dollars each year designing cars and competing on circuits around the globe. They have access to loads of data that can help fine-tune the cars. It's all in the aim of landing atop the podium on a Grand Prix Sunday.

Like any racing series, Formula One has rules that all teams must follow. They include car measurements, safety requirements, and more. This is the "formula" of racing from which the series gets its name.

However, just because everyone plays by the rules doesn't mean that the cars all turn out the same. Formula One cars are all open-wheel, open-cockpit racers. But beneath the surface they are different. Each team looks for its own competitive edge and design components that will help outperform the competition. The way a team designs and builds its car is its main strategy for the season.

THE PLANNING STAGES

The top Formula One teams are backed by luxury car companies or huge corporations that are willing to spend

Formula One cars can be adjusted each week for the challenges of specific tracks, such as the famous tight corners at the Monaco Grand Prix.

whatever it takes to finish first. But money isn't the only factor. Designing a car for a Formula One season is a difficult task.

Compared with IndyCar, Formula One tracks are wildly different. They vary in length, number of turns, top speed,

ORACLE
Red Bull
Mobil 1
BYBIT
Tezos

and more. Teams must design a car that can compete on each course.

Formula One cars are highly adjustable, though. Teams use their practice time before each race testing the car on the track and fine-tuning its setup. One of the main things a team gauges ahead of each race is the aerodynamics of the car.

Formula One cars generate a lot of downforce, which is the effect of air pushing the car to the ground. The amount of downforce can be changed by tweaking the car's setup. Some tracks feature fewer corners; therefore races are run at higher speeds. On these tracks, a team might set up its car with less downforce. That means it will go faster but be harder to turn. In a race with more corners, a high downforce setup will help a car stick to the track in those areas. However, that will cost the car some speed.

Formula One teams plan each race week for how many pit stops they think

Red Bull driver Sergio Perez's crew changes his tires during a 2022 race.

will be needed. This plan has a lot to do with tires. Formula One teams have their choice of three types of tires on a race weekend. Tires range from soft to hard. Softer tires have more

TIRE STRATEGIES AT THE BRITISH GRAND PRIX (52 LAPS)

STRATEGY 1 – ONE PIT STOP

Red (soft tires): 18–22 laps

White (hard tires): 30–34 laps

STRATEGY 2 – TWO PIT STOPS

Red (soft tires): 16–18 laps

Red (soft tires): 16–18 laps

Yellow (medium tires): 16–20 laps

STRATEGY 3 – ONE PIT STOP

Yellow (medium tires): 21–24 laps

White (hard tires): 28–31 laps

grip but wear out more quickly. There are also intermediate and full wet tires for rainy conditions.

To execute a race plan, teams usually mix these tires. They may start off with soft tires to put down some fast laps. They might then switch to hard tires to finish out the race. Another team might make three stops and take soft tires each time. Whatever the plan, it must be followed carefully. Unplanned stops often cost a car any chance at winning the race.

THE GREEN FLAG

In-race strategy is huge in Formula One. And teams must react to changes very quickly. One thing they do not have to worry about is fuel. Refueling isn't allowed during a Formula One race. But as cars burn fuel and become lighter, they handle differently. Teams have to plan for those changes.

Caution flags are uncommon in Formula One. Teams usually expect to make pit stops under green flags, meaning they will lose time to other cars on the track. Pit stops often take less than three seconds. But the total time a car spends on pit road coming in and out can mean a loss of 30 seconds of track time.

Because of this, teams are very careful about when they decide to pit. There are two basic pit strategies—the undercut and the overcut. In an undercut, a team pits before a rival to get newer tires and be able to go faster. In an overcut, a team takes a pit stop later. The hope is that by then the driver has built a large lead. That way opponents can't make up enough ground during the pit stop. Teams want to hide their plan for as long as possible. Racers are always trying to guess what others will do.

Something unexpected can throw a race strategy out the window quickly. A crash can mean one of three things: Cars must slow down near the spot of the accident, all cars must slow down around the whole track, or a safety car comes out to lead the cars around the track at an even slower pace. Each of these means a different length of pit stop as teams scramble to decide what adjustments to make.

THE BIG PICTURE

While Formula One drivers go all out to win the drivers' championship, their teams are competing too. Formula One awards a manufacturers' championship for the team

A collision on the track might change a team's pit-stop strategy during a Formula One race.

ROLEX
ROLEX
ROLEX
ALPHATAURI
Ferrari
cognizant
aramco
cognizant
JCB
aramco
PETRONAS

Max Verstappen, *right,* holds off Lewis Hamilton, *left,* on the final lap of the 2021 Abu Dhabi Grand Prix.

whose two drivers perform best during the season. For that reason, teamwork can be a bigger part of Formula One than in other series.

It is not uncommon for teams to order one driver to let their teammate pass. This usually happens if the trailing driver has a faster car and a better shot at winning. Teams may also order drivers not to race each other too aggressively. A crash between the two could be devastating to a team's chances.

Teams must also remember that the season is long. Rules limit how often teams can change parts of the car such as engines. A team that exceeds the limit might start the race at the back of the pack as a penalty. But that could be worth the risk if the alternative was leaving the faulty part in place and seeing it fail.

Since its Formula One debut in 2005, Red Bull Racing has been one of the strongest teams on the grid. That is due in large part to strategy. A call to change tires late in the 2021 Abu Dhabi Grand Prix meant driver Max Verstappen was in position to run down leader Lewis Hamilton on the last lap, which clinched Verstappen's first world championship. Risks don't always work out, but the upside can mean a trophy.

Team Orders

A decision such as asking one driver to let a teammate pass is known as a team order. Team orders are controversial in Formula One. The 2008 Singapore Grand Prix featured one of the biggest controversies. Nelson Piquet Jr. was ordered to crash deliberately in order to bring out a safety car and let teammate Fernando Alonso take the lead via other teams pitting. The move paid off. Alonso went on to win.

Chapter 4

Endurance Racing

After nearly a full day of racing at the 1966 24 Hours of Daytona, Ken Miles almost saw all of his and teammate Lloyd Ruby's hard work vanish for nothing. He held the lead, but it was shrinking. Miles's team was worried about pushing the car too hard and failing to reach the finish line. As a result, other racers were catching up.

However, when Miles looked toward pit road, he saw a sign on a chalkboard from his team. It was telling him to give the car all it could take. Miles put the throttle down on his Ford GT and blew away the competition

Lloyd Ruby, *left*, and Ken Miles, *right*, celebrate after winning the 24 Hours of Daytona in 1966.

98
98

to win the race. Endurance racing often comes down to knowing when to get aggressive.

THE LONG HAUL

Endurance racing is a unique form of auto racing. Endurance competitions are designed to last a certain number of hours, from six up to 24, such as at Daytona. To win at Daytona, a car must be on the lead lap when the allotted time is complete. At that point, the car that crosses the finish line first wins the race. At the famous 24 hours of Le Mans, the car that has covered the most distance in the allotted time is the winner. So the goal is still to go fast and finish first. But speed is not everything. The car also must survive running throughout the whole race. If a team doesn't make it to the finish line, it doesn't matter how good its lap times were.

THE MARATHON DE LA ROUTE

The longest endurance race ever was the Marathon de la Route. Competitors raced for 84 hours around the famous Nürburgring track in Germany. The grueling race was contested annually for seven years, from 1965 to 1971.

Endurance racing was one of the first forms of auto racing. Before tracks were built specifically for races, competitors drove from city to city in events that

Racers have been competing in endurance races since the early 1900s. The 24 Hours of Le Mans was first run in 1923.

covered hundreds of miles. That tradition continues today in some locations around the world.

There are several different classes and series for endurance racing. The fastest cars are race cars, designed specifically for endurance racing. But there are also high-performance sports cars not all that different from models sold to the public. In endurance races, cars race only against others in their same class.

There are two main endurance racing series. The SportsCar Championship runs in the United States and Canada. The World Endurance Championship races all over the world. In both series, the length of races varies. The most famous endurance races are some of the longest. Every year fans swarm to Florida to watch the 24 Hours of Daytona race. The same thing happens in France for the 24 Hours of Le Mans.

A TEAM APPROACH

An endurance racing season is unlike that of most other racing series. Teams usually employ several drivers in a season. Short races require only two drivers, while 24-hour races often require four or more.

The Meyer Shank Racing team that won the 2023 race at Daytona used four drivers. Two of them, Helio Castroneves and Simon Pagenaud, were IndyCar drivers. Endurance teams often bring in drivers who race in other series for the most important races.

Teams assign a certain portion of the race for each driver to handle. Deciding how long each should drive and when to switch drivers are crucial strategic decisions. Teams want their drivers to stay fresh and ready. But they also want to stick with a driver who is running well. Driving sessions usually last an hour to 90 minutes.

The basic strategy decision endurance racing teams are trying to make is simple: speed vs. longevity. Drivers who go all out from the start of the race will wear out the car, tires,

Teammates Robin Frijns, *left,* Stuart Leonard, *center,* and Dries Vanthoor pose on the podium after winning a 12-hour endurance race in Australia in 2018.

and fuel. Instead they must take a balanced approach. With so much time on the track, they also must be careful to avoid incidents with other racers.

It is often better to drop back from the pack if there is a chance of being involved in a wreck. Over the course of an entire day of racing, drivers have plenty of time to make up those seconds. However, drivers must also know the right time to push the car and make up ground or extend a lead.

Fuel mileage is tricky in endurance racing. Teams can never be totally sure how long the fuel will last. Often, they estimate based on time instead of by distance. Car fuel mileage might also vary during different stages of the race, as sometimes the car will be pushed harder. Knowing when to make that last pit stop can be the difference between winning and losing.

Pit stop speed is not quite as important in a race measured by hours, but teams have one extra thing to contend with—changing drivers. Getting one driver unbuckled and out, and the new one in, does take some time. One thing that makes it easier is that drivers carry a seat insert designed for their height so they don't need to move the seat at all.

Endurance racing is a specific challenge, but all forms of motorsports have their share of those. Whatever the

A Tiny Fraction of 24 Hours

The 2023 version of the 24 Hours of Daytona proved that no second can be taken for granted, even in a marathon race. In the LMP-2 racing class, the checkered flag came down to a photo finish. James Allen from the Proton Competition team won by just .016 seconds.

Teams make pit stops in the dark during the 24 hours of Daytona race in 2023.

form of vehicle, strategy plays a part in any type of racing. Often it is the team that did its homework that will take the checkered flag.

GLOSSARY

aerodynamics

The forces of air moving around an object.

caution flag

A flag waved to indicate an accident on the track.

chassis

The main part of a car, where the engine and suspension are attached.

checkered flag

A flag waved to indicate the end of a race.

Grand Prix

From the French for "grand prize," any race that is part of the Formula One championship series.

green flag

A flag waved to indicate the start of a race, or a resumption of full racing after a caution period.

horsepower

A measurement of power in a vehicle.

open-wheel

A car with the wheels outside the vehicle's main body.

pit stop

A stop during a race to change tires or make repairs to a car.

road course

A closed road course designed to simulate public roads.

sports car

A two-door vehicle designed for speed or racing.

suspension

The system on a vehicle designed to absorb bumps in a road.

MORE INFORMATION

Books

Hustad, Douglas. *Innovations in Auto Racing*. Minneapolis, MN: Abdo Publishing, 2022.

Rule, Heather. *Formula One Teams*. Minneapolis, MN: Abdo Publishing, 2024.

Rule, Heather. *GOATs of Auto Racing*. Minneapolis, MN: Abdo Publishing, 2022.

Online Resources

To learn more about auto racing strategies, please visit **abdobooklinks.com** or scan this QR code. These links are routinely monitored and updated to provide the most current information available.

INDEX

About the Author

Anthony K. Hewson is a freelance writer originally from San Diego. He and his wife now live in the San Francisco Bay Area with their two dogs.